50 FAVORITE ROOMS BY
FRANK LLOYD WRIGHT

YE'VE LEFT A GLIMMER STILL TO CHEER
THE MAN—THE ARTIFEX
THAT HOLDS IN SPITE O'KNOCKS AND SCALE
O'FRICTION WASTE AN'SLIP,
AN'BY THAT LIGHT—NOW MARK MY WORD—
WE'LL BUILD THE PERFECT SHIP.

50 FAVORITE ROOMS BY FRANK LLOYD WRIGHT

DIANE MADDEX

ABRADALE PRESS

HARRY N. ABRAMS, INC., PUBLISHERS

Produced by Archetype Press, Inc.

Project Director: Diane Maddex

Editorial Assistants: Gretchen Smith Mui and John Hovanec

Designer: Robert L. Wiser

This book was composed in Bernhard Gothic, designed by Lucian
Bernhard in 1929 for American Type Founders. The display typography
is Wade Sans, designed by Paul Hickson in 1990 for Esselte Letraset.

Endpapers and chapter dividers: The fret-sawn panel in the dining room of
the Frank Lloyd Wright Home and Studio (1889–95), Oak Park, Illinois

Page 2: The drafting room of Wright's Oak Park studio (1898)

The Library of Congress has cataloged the Abrams edition as follows:

Maddex, Diane.

50 favorite rooms by Frank Lloyd Wright / Diane Maddex.

p.   cm.

"An Archetype Press book."

Includes bibliographical references and index.

ISBN 0-7651-0839-9 (alk. paper)

1. Wright, Frank Lloyd, 1867–1959—Criticism and interpretation.

2. Interior architecture—United States. 3. Room layout (Dwellings)—

United States. I. Title.

NA737.W7M28 1998

720'.92—dc21   98-7285

Abradale ISBN 0-8109-8211-0

Printed in Singapore

10   9   8   7   6   5   4   3   2

Abradale Press

Harry N. Abrams, Inc.

100 Fifth Avenue

New York, NY 10011

www.abramsbooks.com

Abrams is a subsidiary of

LA MARTINIÈRE
G R O U P E

INTRODUCTION

Over a career spanning seven decades, Frank Lloyd Wright designed about one thousand buildings. Only half of these were built (the others were his "children of imagination"), but taking a conservative average of eight rooms each—six in small houses, ten or more in larger residences, plus scores in his offices and public buildings—he may have produced four thousand livable rooms, perhaps five thousand including miscellaneous spaces. They came to him so easily, he said, that he merely shook them out of his sleeve. In a single decade launching the twentieth century, he churned out some one hundred fifty ideas. In the last sixteen years of his life, well into his ninety-second year, he completed five hundred designs.

How can fifty of these rooms represent such a heroic output? And which fifty illustrate the reach of Wright's imagination, which took different paths and roads less traveled by as he sought a new architecture for a new age? In his long lifespan, Wright produced many versions of what he termed "organic architecture." The Prairie style of the century's first decade, the California textile-block houses of the 1920s, the one-of-a-kind 1930s designs such as Fallingwater, and the Usonian houses that predominated during the 1940s and 1950s are all manifestations of his unwavering principles of simplicity, unity, and respect for nature. Favorites—because they either clearly epitomize Wright's goals or strike a personal emotional chord—have been chosen by scholars and amateurs for years. One could almost take any fifty rooms across the wide spectrum of his work, but the spaces here clearly show that for Wright

the room became the essential expression of architecture. From the genius of their conception to the brilliance of their execution, these examples stand as tangible proof that simple recognition of human needs can produce a living architecture. Except for a few that survive mainly on paper, these favorites are also among the best preserved of Wright's work and thus continue to give the pleasure that he always intended.

Wright himself has become probably the world's favorite architect of the twentieth century, although he was born in the nineteenth century—in 1867 in Richland Center, Wisconsin—and died four decades ago in 1959. His continuing favor with the public may stem in great part from the simple fact that he preferred to design houses. Unlike so many contemporary architects whose fame rests on structures for everything but living in, Wright saw himself destined to be a residential architect. For him, the family in the home was the basic unit of society and modern democracy.

Wright's idealism was nurtured in the Wisconsin countryside, in the hills and farms belonging to the Lloyd Jones family of his mother, Anna Lloyd Wright. From them and from his father, William Russell Carey Wright, a preacher and musician, he learned the principles of Unitarianism and the unity of all things, which he was to translate into his own buildings. His father also imbued in him a love of music, while his mother set his sights on architecture. She gave him a gift that lasted him a lifetime: geometric blocks and spatial teaching tools developed

Palmer House (1952), Ann Arbor, Michigan

by the German educator Friedrich Froebel. The cubes, triangles, and spheres with which he spent his childhood were to emerge transformed as buildings and as the overriding motifs inside them. The heart of nature itself, their geometry underlay nearly every idea that came from his drafting table. In the fields that he worked and studied as a boy, Wright found the roots of an organic architecture—one in which a building could grow from its own needs just as a plant rises from the soil, "as free to be itself…as is the tree."

Wright preferred to study nature rather than engineering, so he left the University of Wisconsin in 1887 and became an architect first by apprenticing at the age of twenty with Joseph Lyman Silsbee and then with Louis Sullivan, the noted Chicago School designer of skyscrapers and exquisite ornament. On his own after 1893, Wright found his voice in several commissions that burst on the scene with the shock of the new. Between the time he designed his first Prairie house in 1900 and his weary departure for Europe nine years later, he discovered the secret of designing rooms that nourished the spirit and thereby etched his name in architectural history.

When he became an architect, Wright saw popular interior layouts—Victorians and period revivals—as nothing but boxes beside or inside other boxes, which people called rooms. Each human function had its own box, sequestered away from other boxes like cells in penal institutions. He wanted nothing to do with pasted-on pastiches of old styles, and he spent the remainder of his career tearing down walls that blocked true freedom of movement. After he designed the Larkin Building in Buffalo in 1903 and began work the next year on Unity Temple in his hometown of Oak Park outside Chicago, a revelation came to him: Unity's interior needs could shape the whole edifice, so that the rooms inside would dictate the architecture outside. As he later put it, the "enclosed space within" became the reality of the building. The room itself was the crucial determinant, one manifested on the exterior by the requirements of the interior.

Homes in particular, Wright concluded, should be not caves but shelters. "I saw a house, primarily, as a livable interior space under ample shelter," he wrote in *The Natural House* in 1954. Viewing houses as clumsy counterparts of the human body, he set out to rid them of the indigestion gnawing at the stomach—the interior. Wright began by eliminating the insignificant, a process of simplification similar to the Japanese woodblock prints that he admired and collected. First of all, he reduced the number of rooms to the fewest necessary for comfort and utility. One large room on the first floor of a house would have been enough for him, but it took Wright several decades to persuade clients of this. As walls came down, replaced by large openings and legerdemain instead of doors, rooms borrowed space from one another, making each seem larger. Outer walls themselves turned into screens, the solid masonry or wood of old replaced more and more by windows grouped together to form continuous bands of light and air.

In his continuous quest for everything that was simple, unified, and natural, Wright developed solutions that were revolutionary:

For simplicity, machines and standardization allowed new economies of scale. Unnecessary rooms gave way to combined uses in larger open spaces. Doors and windows stopped being holes in walls and became part of the structure. Integral ornament took the place of applied decoration. Furniture was often built in to conserve space. Two-dimensional pictures and cluttering objects were banished. Mechanical equipment was hidden away. A sense of repose suffused every corner.

For unity, each building used its own grammar—a plan or motif that governed every architectural and decorative aspect of how it spoke to the world. Furnishings were fully coordinated with the architecture, adding to the harmony of the whole.

For the love of nature, Wright's buildings appeared to grow easily from their sites and respected their surroundings. Terraces and expanses of glass brought the outdoors inside, aided by bouquets of dried flowers or weeds. Roofs paralleled the ground to epitomize shelter. Colors emulated the woods and fields. Materials were used pure, as nature intended. And everywhere, geometry synthesized nature to its very essence.

In these fifty rooms, Wright's precepts come directly to life— expressions of beauty true to their time and place and thus, as Wright demanded, "architecture that we can call organic."

9

Frank Lloyd Wright at Taliesin West in 1947

LIVING

For Wright, the living room was the heart of the home. In fact, he said

in 1908, it was the only important room that any house really needed.

Some basic requirements—the kitchen, servants' quarters, bedrooms—

should be hidden away from it, but all other domestic activities, screened

by "architectural contrivances," could take place in this pivotal space.

ROOMS

A built-in bench invited reading, the fireplace encouraged conversation, broad

banks of windows inspired contemplation, a table in an alcove allowed dining

in place, and nature beckoned from a garden. In the absence of doors and high

walls, open vistas permitted the eye to travel naturally from one end of the

house to the other. Wright simplified family life as he simplified his buildings.

FRANK LLOYD WRIGHT HOME AND STUDIO

Early in his career, Wright liked to say that he learned more by redoing his own home and workplace than by designing anything else. The house he built in 1889 in Oak Park, Illinois, to celebrate his marriage to Catherine Tobin thus became his most trusted and productive laboratory. He fussed with it constantly, at first just rearranging the furnishings but then remodeling the house significantly in 1895 and soon building a studio for himself in 1898. As he pushed and pulled everything from walls and windows to small sculptures, he jelled the ideas that were to define a lifetime of creativity. Although the triangular front gable seems strikingly modern, the shingled house inside and out at first owed more to lingering Victorian ideas than to the new design principles Wright was to foster. In the living room, diamond-paned windows and dentil moldings were architectural holdovers, while new electric light bulbs affixed to swirling Sullivanesque ceiling panels merely bridged past and future. But Wright moved quickly to break away from dated design theories by creating a fully unified environment. Borrowing from Arts and Crafts ideals, he tucked a cozy fireside inglenook, complete with a homily, into the room. Upholstered benches reappear in a luxurious expanse of built-in sofa under the bay windows, eliminating the need for much bulky freestanding furniture. Pillows add spots of color, which are picked up in oriental rugs that define walkways. Pale green and gold tones bring nature inside, aided by landscape paintings. Wright himself designed comfortable chairs with spindled arms and a clever table to display his precious Japanese prints. Simplicity, the forms and textures of nature, a singular vision—many of Wright's innovations took place here in his own living room.

DANA-THOMAS HOUSE

By 1902, when Wright designed this very social house in Springfield, Illinois, for the heiress Susan Lawrence Dana, he had already made a name for himself and was embarked on a decade-long race to fill clients' requests for more and more Prairie houses. Yet even in the half century of work left to him, he was seldom to receive such a free hand and lavish budget. The result was a glorious ode to joy played out in glass and light, mystery and freedom. Spaces such as this gallery for exhibitions and soirées soar two stories high, crowned by a barrel vault ribbed in wood. The arch motif here is first announced at the front entrance, then carried in one direction to the dining room and another to this end of the luxurious house designed for entertaining. Like a moon rising, the window at the far end presents the overriding pattern Wright used to unify his composition: prairie sumac, abstracted and synthesized to its geometric essence. This native plant grows throughout the house in glimmering art glass windows and light fixtures, making each room appear to be "cut from one piece of goods," just as Wright liked. More sumac climbs a novel music cabinet, while two of the architect's print tables allow undivided attention for one of his favorite pastimes. Behind them, an enclosed sofa creates a snug room within the room. In this ensemble, not a false note can be heard.

ROBIE HOUSE

The consummate expression of Wright's Prairie style, the Robie House in Chicago almost defies description. The noted architectural historian Henry-Russell Hitchcock wavered between calling the 1908 design an airplane and "a great ship carrying the world of nature, as well as the world of abstract space, into the urban commonplaceness of Hyde Park." He likened the living and dining spaces on the second floor, perched high above the ground, to an ocean liner's public rooms, encircled by light-filled decks. The two rooms form one continuous space, interrupted only by the staircase and a massive fireplace of Roman brick. At either end are shiplike "prows," triangular projections for fine vistas. Heavy walls have given way to screens of glass that bring the outside in but keep it distant with a delicate pattern. Here Wright chose a geometric version of a flower framing a stylized version of the house's own plan. Above the windows dramatic wood bands, punctuated by rotund spheres of light, urge the walls and ceiling to flow together into one plastic space. The bulbs shine down on a carpet whose quiet pattern was woven especially to reflect the interior themes, all of which were coordinated by the interior designer George Niedecken, one of Wright's associates. From square stools and a sofa whose arms cantilever outward like the wings of the house, the furniture underscored the horizontal sweep at the core of the Prairie style itself. For Wright, the horizontal line was the line of domesticity.

MAY HOUSE

A hearth was the home for Wright—the symbol of warmth and center of family activities. Often one was not enough to satisfy this primeval need for a fire burning deep in the masonry of the house itself. For the family of Sophie and Meyer May, a clothier in Grand Rapids, Michigan, Wright carved an exceptional fireplace out of their 1908 living room. A slash of stone for a mantel, integrated with the wall rather than pasted on, and deeply raked, narrow Roman brick accentuate the horizontality of the prairie. Between the bricks he spun glass into fiery gold, glazing the mortar to reflect the golden hues of the room. Perpendicular to the hearth, a padded bench backed by bookshelves invites reading or daydreaming. Without boxy walls, spaces borrow from one another and views meander in all directions—through a delicate oak screen and around a pillar, temporarily resting on a hollyhock mural by George Niedecken in the hall outside the dining room. The seamless flow of space makes the house seem larger than it is, a relatively modest commission for a midwestern family. Subdued autumn colors and soft textures add a sense of calm and repose, creating a private retreat that embodies the idea of home.

TALIESIN

Wright's second home, built on family land in the rolling
hills near Spring Green, Wisconsin, was a work in progress
over five decades of his life, beginning in 1911. His architectural
experimentation here stemmed from desire as well as sheer
necessity—parts of the house at Taliesin burned not once
but twice, in 1914 and 1925, the first time engulfing his mistress,
Mamah Borthwick Cheney, her two children, and four others
in a madman's inferno. Wright's "shining brow" (*taliesin* in
Welsh) was reborn, better and larger with each rebuilding.
Rough courses of local limestone cladding the exterior come
indoors, blurring the distinction between the natural world
and the secluded universe within. Stone meets wood as the
two meet in the landscape nearby. Colored like sand from
the riverbank below, smooth plaster softens walls and the
ceiling, which rises to a crescendo marked by thin wood strips
that create flat planes of color. Within this tented cathedral
of a living room, mirroring the sloping hills outside, horizontal
wood bands dance around the space as ledges for objects,
high window sills, trim on low dividers, and edges of tabletops
and footstools. The sense of movement is palpable; the eye
does not know where to rest. Zoned areas help lead the
way to a dining alcove or to built-in seating around the
limestone hearth. Indirect lighting makes the room glow, and
golden features such as oriental screens pick up the theme.
Originally much more rectilinear, the dining chairs were
replaced in the 1930s with barrel chairs like the ones Wright
designed for the Martin House in Buffalo, New York, one
of his Prairie masterpieces. Sunlight, warmed by the music
of birds and the scent of blossoms, comes through the open
windows. Completing the inspired composition are some
of the sculptures and objects that Wright collected and
prized for their own three-dimensional quality.

LITTLE HOUSE

Viewed as a coda to Wright's prolific Prairie years, the house he designed in 1912 for Francis and Mary Little beside Lake Minnetonka in Minnesota was a finale only such a master could compose. The living room—and this is nearly all that remains, as the house has been demolished—towers over mere mortals below. Progressing ever higher, from transom level to the ceiling band, then almost bursting into the sky, the room epitomizes the Prairie sense of shelter. Parallel bands of wood stretch across the ceiling its full fifty-foot length, merging with the golden skylight in the center. More glass sparkles beneath, from a clerestory row down to tall windows that once looked out over the lake but now see only the inside of the Metropolitan Museum of Art in New York City. Triangular patterns float around the glass edges, leaving the center clear for unobstructed views. A window seat provided the perfect perch. Mary Little used the room as a concert hall, which helps explain why it resembles an edifice of sound like the symphonies Wright's father taught him to love. The Littles had previously owned another Wright house, built in Peoria, Illinois, in 1903, and they brought some of its furniture with them. Wright had already moved beyond his designs of a decade earlier and would have preferred to give them completely new items created just for this space. But the strong horizontal planes of both the furniture and the built-in wood decks suit each other well. For decoration, Wright urged his clients to bring nature inside in the form of dried leaves or even weeds. The Littles apparently also adopted one of Wright's two favorite sculptures, the *Winged Victory*. In his own living room in Oak Park he displayed a bust of Beethoven, showing that his too was a musical household.

HOLLYHOCK HOUSE

Reinventing himself after the Prairie years, Wright turned
architecture into Romance with a capital *R* on a hill in Hollywood. He called this commission a natural house, free in form
and native to the region. Its sometime occupant was Aline
Barnsdall, an oil heiress with a restless spirit. She adored hollyhocks and, said Wright, called on him to render them "as a
feature of Architecture how I might." And how he did! His 1917
design planted them in a ring around the templelike facade
and scattered them asymmetrically on windows; he had them
climb up the backs of chairs and cascade down interior walls, all
using squares in his inimitable stylized fashion. More geometric
motifs—circles, diamonds, and spindles—energize the dramatic
overmantel in the living room. Sandwiched between a skylighted hood and a golden pool, the fireplace speaks of fire and
water, earth and air. Surrounding it is an elaborate built-in sofa
with tables and torchieres. Golden walls provide the only
frames the Japanese screens need. Throughout the "proud
house"—in the art glass, for example—Wright introduced a new
color palette appropriate for California's sunnier locale. Purple
and green were a far cry from the autumnal harvest colors of
his Prairie houses but a taste of more surprises to come.

LA MINIATURA

Wright was busy in the early 1920s overseeing construction
of his famed Imperial Hotel in Tokyo but not too busy—he did
not in fact have much other work—to seek ways of stretching
the possibilities of common building materials and methods.
He turned to concrete, developing his own interlocking system
of precast blocks that could stack up into secure exterior walls
while they offered integral ornament on the inside. Wright
compared his new technique to weaving a rug and called
his material textile blocks. Standardization was his goal—to
streamline the construction process while using machines to
produce infinite variety. A quartet of houses in the Los Angeles
area still testify to the master weaver's skill. For Alice Millard
of Pasadena, a former client in Illinois, he designed a house in
1923 that grew like a cactus in a challenging ravine, a tall structure different from his ground-hugging commissions of the
Midwest. The textured blocks, he boasted, would make the
site's eucalyptus trees more beautiful. Millard asked Wright
only to give her a large living room, a great fireplace, and a
balcony opening onto her bedroom. Above the ravine-level
dining room rises an appropriately dramatic two-story living
room whose walls need few embellishments. The same pattern
used for the exterior, a cross motif, works inside to subtly blend
indoors and out. Mixed in with the decorative blocks are plain
ones and some that are pierced to add light and shadow, much
like the windows. In a house built for views, with terraces from
the ground to the roof, the living room balcony seems wholly
at home. It helps bring the space down to human level, where
a hearth adds its own glow to the magical blocks. Even after
a trying construction process—in which the builder was fired,
the roof leaked, a flood damaged the house, and technological
problems intervened—Wright contended that he would rather
have designed this miniature gem than St. Peter's in Rome.

28

STORER HOUSE

Wright teased that concrete "lived mostly in the architectural gutter," but he knew how to use this cheap and ugly building material (as he phrased it) to startling effect. For the second of his four textile-block houses in California, built for John Storer in Hollywood in 1923, Wright wove the walls with eleven distinctive patterns. The sheer number of choices, all based on overlapping squares, made for seemingly endless variations: pierced and plain, projecting and receding, horizontal rows, vertical stacks, solid walls, screens of light. Wright's tapestry had many stories to tell. In the tall living room, raised to the second story as at La Miniatura, the blocks cast rich shadows and stake out a fireplace that reaches to the ceiling like a wall containing a flame. At either end are terraces that open the house to the outside and offer views of Hollywood and Los Angeles beyond. The *Winged Victory*, always a favorite of the architect, suggests the lightness of air, but Wright made sure that this house, unlike Millard's, stayed well anchored by adding steel reinforcing rods to produce blocks as strong as they were picturesque.

FALLINGWATER

No house embodies Wright's ideas as well as Fallingwater, the vacation retreat cantilevered over a waterfall in Mill Run, Pennsylvania. An exceptional site and exceptional clients came together with daring genius to produce a masterwork, now one of the most famous houses in the world. Wright was sixty-seven years old in 1934, when Edgar and Liliane Kaufmann decided to have him build a weekend home on their rugged site. If they expected the house to be merely near their favorite waterfall, they underestimated their architect. Instead, it emerges from the native stone and cascades over the spilling water as if it were nature itself— "of the hill," not on the hill, as Wright always demanded. Deep concrete terraces reach out like stacked dominoes to embrace the spectacular site, coaxing light and shade inside. In the living room wide expanses of glass outlined in red frame changing views to rival any landscape painting. The immense, forty-eight-foot-long space is zoned into secluded corners for different activities that suited the Kaufmanns' informal weekends: eating, reading, writing, or just enjoying the scenery. Wright placed furniture along the room's edges, cantilevering sofas and walnut tables to recall Fallingwater's signature terraces outside. Like leaves falling in the ravine, orange and yellow cushions punctuate the earth tones of the local sandstone. The waxed stone floor shows that nature is underfoot, close but held just at bay by Wright's magic. It is a house, suggests the critic Paul Goldberger, that "summed up the 20th century and then thrust it forward still further."

HANNA HOUSE

In the mid-1930s Wright began addressing what he regarded
as America's major architectural problem: the house of
moderate cost. He called his solution Usonian—after Samuel
Butler's name for the United States—and tailored his new
designs to the informal American lifestyle. To reduce the
cost of labor and materials, Wright's Usonian houses relied
on geometric modules, or plans, and standardized components.
For Paul and Jean Hanna of Palo Alto, California, Wright
in 1936 tried out a new module, a hexagon. Octagons and
of course squares and rectangles occupied secure places
in his architectural vocabulary, but the hexagon seemed to
hold out more potential for relaxed angles. In the Hannas'
living room the hexagonal plan of the house is telegraphed
immediately by small details: the projection of the fireplace,
the stepped brick hearth, red and blue hexagons suspended
on the grate, colorful footstools, and seat backs mounted over
the built-in bench. Beneath all, the concrete floor is inscribed
with hexagons to reinforce the message. The unit system,
combined with flexible walls and other economical building
techniques, helped launch Wright on the road to Usonia and
new modules such as the triangle. Wright himself compared
this ground-breaking plan to a bee's honeycomb, and to this
day it is often known by its nickname, Honeycomb House.

TALIESIN WEST

As much as he loved pastoral Wisconsin, Wright came to be seduced by the desert of Arizona. He first fell under its spell in 1927, when he journeyed west to work on the Arizona Biltmore Hotel and then two years later to begin an ill-fated resort project that died with the Great Depression. At that time Wright improvised a camp shaded by translucent canvas roofs and named it after the ocatillo cactus flower. Like the desert, the seed of the idea for the roofs was firmly planted and took root when Wright came back to the Phoenix area in 1937 to start a permanent winter home for himself and his Taliesin Fellowship of architects, founded in 1932. Instead of box boards, this time he collected more enduring boulders and set them into concrete to create rubble walls entirely in harmony with the desert site, now a part of Scottsdale. For his "desert ships," Wright stretched peaked canvas sails between redwood trusses angled to reflect the McDowell Mountains behind the property. More poetic than practical, the canvas roofs eventually were replaced with synthetic materials. But the soaring ceilings visible today in spaces such as the garden room retain the natural quality—akin to butterflies lighting on a desert rock—that Wright so admired. His chosen geometric motif here was the triangle, in homage to the mountains. In the rise of the roof, a decorative screen, a hanging sculpture, and tables and chairs, peaked forms bring these natural wonders indoors. The famous plywood chairs here, in Wright's original sitting room, have been compared to Japanese origami, as if they had been deftly folded and presented to guests. Lines of built-in benches, backed by walls of desert stone, add a rectangular counterpoint and anchor the lofty structure in which Wright spent his last two decades.

WINGSPREAD

If ever there were doubts about Wright's reverence for
the hearth, they would be put to rest in the living area
of this sprawling house near Racine, Wisconsin. Completed
in 1939, Wingspread is what its name implies—a pinwheel
whose four wings revolve around a central core as if poised
for flight. At the heart of the house, pushing thirty-eight feet
toward the freedom of the sky, is Wright's all-purpose chimney
stack. Its five fireplaces serve and set apart the activity spheres
of the Great Hall: entry, living area, library, music alcove, and
dining room, which are further marked by changing levels.
Sinuously curved, the brick monolith disappears into a unique
octagonal roof ringed by three tiers of clerestory windows.
An oak mezzanine, complete with a spiraling stair to a glassed-
in observation deck, helps bring the three-story space back
down to human level. The rotund black kettle nestling inside
the fireplace was a Wright trademark and has a match in red
at Fallingwater and other houses of the period. Barrel chairs
similar to those designed originally for the Martin House pick
up the circular theme. Coffee tables, end tables, and footstools
appeared as hexagons, giving Wright yet another opportunity
to transform his childhood Froebel blocks into architectural
geometry. Wingspread was the home of Herbert F. Johnson,
president of the Johnson Wax Company, who lived as well as
worked in buildings designed by Wright. Today it is a conference
center and headquarters of the Johnson Foundation.

CEDAR ROCK

After inventing Usonian houses in the mid-1930s, Wright spent the next decade perfecting them. All were "parallel to the ground, companion to the horizon." Roofs became flat, and garages were turned into carports. Gutters and downspouts disappeared, along with basements, interior trim, plaster, paint, radiators, light fixtures—anything that cluttered. Furniture was built in or built to fit in. "A cultured American housewife," suggested Wright, would look well in one. In Quasqueton, Iowa, he was handed a site in 1945 only a shade less inspiring than Fallingwater's. Projecting above a bend in the Wapsipinicon River, Agnes and Lowell Walter's remote property called out for glass, and Wright obliged with an adaptation of a Usonian glass house published in the *Ladies' Home Journal*. Gone are solid masonry walls in the living room, called the garden room, and in their place rise windows that make the water and the woods part of the composition. A strip of clerestories above them and, higher still, square skylights invite additional light into the L-shaped room, which is angled from the house to catch the view. Plants thrive in this indoor corner of nature. Below the house on the riverbank, spanning an enormous boulder, is a two-story brick pavilion with space for boats and a terrace for close-up contemplation.

PALMER HOUSE

One of Wright's most welcoming Usonian houses was designed in 1950 for a couple who loved music as much as he. Mary and William Palmer actually shared a musical evening with their architect and friends in their new home in Ann Arbor, Michigan, several years after it was built in 1952. Wright's instrument of choice here was the triangle, arranged in a series to form the plan of the house. A combined dining and living area fills the point of the largest triangle, a theme repeated from the peak of the glowing cypress ceiling down to the waxed red concrete floor that hides heating coils underfoot. (Wright considered naked radiators an abomination.) Wood decks encircle the space, hiding indirect lights to soften them and offering ledges to display reminders of nature. Triangular stools underscore the triangular grammar of the house. Golden flowers blossom on the dining chairs to add a Japanese sensibility completely in tune with Wright's work. An oriental serenity continues outside, as the wall of glass opens onto a terrace and a garden beyond. There the Palmers in 1964 added a Japanese tea house that enriches the spirit of the house while remaining faithful to Wright's opus.

R. L. WRIGHT HOUSE

When Wright's children were small, he hung balloon-shaped
lights from the ceiling of their playroom in Oak Park. Always
fascinated with circles, Wright increasingly added them
to his architectural vocabulary in the 1950s. Who knows if
childhood balloons came to mind when Wright was asked to
design homes for two sons? David Wright in Arizona received
a rotund circle of concrete block in 1950, while for his youngest son, Robert Llewellyn Wright, and his wife, Elizabeth,
the *paterfamilias* pulled out a balloon pinched at each end.
Designed for a ravine in Bethesda, Maryland, in 1953, the
elliptical house presents a private face to the street but opens
on the opposite side to panoramic vistas. The living room
doors and windows, sandwiched between the ceiling and
a low wall of simple concrete block, form a hemicycle similar
to several other Usonian houses of Wright's. Essentially solar
walls, they bring in light and open up the room to nature.
A circular fireplace helps screen a circular kitchen behind it.
Specially designed footstools and a storage table mirror the
shape of the house itself. They float like boats on a rug whose
colorful circles could be balloons brought down to earth.

RAYWARD HOUSE

For an architect who loved to build with nature, Wright was fortunate that many clients brought him exceptional sites. Nestled in a wooded watershed along a pond, the house in New Canaan, Connecticut, designed for the John L. Rayward family in 1955 was named Tirranna (an Australian word) in appreciation for its waterside setting. Wright chose another hemicycle of glass to frame the spectacular scenery, stretching it from the living area, past the kitchen hidden behind a divider, and into the dining room beyond. Outside, a terrace overlooks a swimming pool, which in turn balances above nature's own pond and waterfall. Rich Philippine mahogany punches up walls of plain concrete block and surrounds the floor-to-ceiling windows, which act as a passive solar collector. Wright recycled several of his furniture designs for the Raywards, including colorful hexagonal nesting tables that first appeared at Taliesin West about 1937 and side chairs with curved, spindled backs. Similar low-back chairs were pulled up around the table in the dining area at the far end of the sunny window wall. In 1955, the year the house was designed, average consumers also were finally able to buy mass-produced furniture designed by Wright when the Heritage-Henredon Furniture Company launched its Taliesin Ensemble of furnishings "for the general homemaker, rather than for special clients," as announced in *House Beautiful*. Tall-back chairs from this commercial line—offering hexagonal tables, triangular stools, oval hassocks, and other items in Wright's favorite geometric shapes—later replaced the Rayward dining chairs. Even if they did not have Tirranna's fine setting or its masterful form, the Heritage-Henredon furniture allowed more homeowners than ever to bring Wright into their own living rooms.

DINING

Dining "always was a great artistic opportunity" for Wright. In one well-defined space, he could unite both the family and his own principles of architecture. Although the form of his dining rooms evolved over the years, he never strayed from the concept of unity. In 1896 he envisioned cheerful rooms that one would "involuntarily enter with a smile" and gave his clients

ROOMS

dramatic rooms within rooms, furnished with high-back chairs sheltering a

massive plank for dining. Set well apart, they remained open to nature and

other domestic preserves. In later years Wright moved the act of dining to the

living area and tucked it into a corner. In doing so, he succeeded in breaking

down the boxy walls of a house that hindered a sense of seamless repose.

FRANK LLOYD WRIGHT HOME AND STUDIO

When Wright remodeled his Oak Park home in 1895,
he gave himself the opportunity to test his rapidly changing
ideas of what architecture should be. The twenty-eight-
year-old architect created an entirely new dining room
in place of the old kitchen—and in one stroke put into play
his principles of simplicity, unity, and the sanctity of natural
materials. The growing Wright family now dined in a space as
perfect as he could make it. High-back oak chairs created a
room of their room, encouraging both formality and reverence
for dining en famille. Even on the high chair for his youngest
son, Llewellyn, slats serve as screens in wood, an idea possibly
inspired by Japanese architecture. No light bulbs intrude;
soft light (Wright called it "moonlight") filters down through
a fret-sawn wood grille recessed into the ceiling. The same
rectangular shape as the table, it is filled with geometric
motifs and began a lifelong interest in pierced and perforated
panels. Natural light comes from windows in the bay. More
intricate than the diamond-paned glass in the original parts of
the house, their delicate pattern stylizes a lotus design from
a pattern book. Grouped together, the windows extend the
walls with a screen of glass that lets diners see out but
discourages prying eyes. In fact, the lower level was filled in
when neighbors moved too close. Cabinets below conceal
radiators. Across the red tile floor is a fireplace to warm family
meals. As uncluttered as Victorian rooms were stuffy, Wright's
new dining room, raved an 1899 account in House Beautiful,
radiated "a golden tone such as one sees in a rich sunset."

WILLITS HOUSE

By 1901, when he designed this house in the Chicago suburb of Highland Park for his friends Ward and Cecilia Willits, Wright's principles had coalesced into an architectural language known as the Prairie style. Other designers practiced it, but he became its master. Sheltering roofs, an overriding sense of horizontality, open plans, natural materials and colors—all came together here, in what he regarded as his first great Prairie house. In the dining room, Wright brought nature indoors. Like a clearing in the forest, trunks of oak stand tall between walls of leafy green. "Moonlight" peeks through the ceiling's magnificent canopy of golden art glass, which is tucked behind intersecting branches of wood. Sunlight streams into the secluded grove from windows on either side and from a triangular bay that projects the room into the landscape. Continuous wall surfaces have almost vanished; in their place is sheer glass that suggests a wall but offers more rewards. At the heart of the room, a rectilinear grouping of table and tall chairs invites intimacy and attention to the meal. Slats in the chairs recall wood screens placed elsewhere in the house to quietly mark divisions of space. The wood pieces widen to run in bands along the walls at ceiling height, tying the room into a unified masterpiece. In a forest such as this, many people would just as soon stay undiscovered.

DANA·THOMAS HOUSE

When the social set of Springfield, Illinois, called on Susan Lawrence Dana in her brand-new home in December 1904, they knew they had entered a different world. Through the arched entry, under butterflies rendered in art glass, past a fountain of "moonchildren," they encountered a serene two-story space in which they were invited to dine like kings and queens right there on the American prairie. For this wealthy widow, Wright had conjured up a near-palace for entertaining, "somewhat elaborately worked out in detail," he admitted with a bit of understatement. The dining room is a prairie feast, served on an autumn palette: a pumpkin ceiling of sand-finished plaster, earthy oak furniture to seat forty guests, four golden chandeliers that could be floating butterflies, all wrapped midway up in George Niedecken's naturalistic mural capturing the native sumac, golden rod, and purple asters that show their colors in the fall. With slats dropping elegantly low to the floor, chairs came in both tall- and short-back versions (the latter for women). Stays of oak in the barrel-vaulted ceiling direct one's gaze back to a breakfast nook recessed in a circular alcove. Built-in benches follow the curve and are lighted naturally by a troupe of exceptional art glass windows dancing above. Here sumac—the unifying motif of the house—grows in profusion. Wright stylized stems and leaves into pure geometry, building up rectangular and triangular pieces of amber and clear glass. They move up and down, sideways, and in angled chevrons to produce a bouquet that was one of Wright's most bountiful gifts in glass.

ROBIE HOUSE

During the first decade of the twentieth century, when Wright churned out scores of Prairie designs, he perfected his idea of what a dining room should be. So that families could dine in repose, the space was separate but not necessarily boxed in by suffocating walls. The table held center stage, surrounded by tall chairs that marked their own room within the larger one. Built-ins eliminated cumbersome freestanding pieces. Windows brought nature inside, but their intricate patterns masked the nakedness of clear glass. All of Wright's concepts came together in his 1906 design for the Robie House in Chicago. Occupying the second floor at the opposite end from the living room, the masterful space presents a seamless transition separated by just a stairway and a fireplace. The same autumnal windows, the same wood banding carrying spherical lights, the same carpeting unifies the two rooms. Verticals and horizontals mingle to nourish the eye and the spirit. At the far end, in the matching "prow," Wright tucked away one of his increasingly common breakfast nooks. When they were dining alone, this is where the Robies preferred to sit—saving the grand stage set in the center of the room for the edification of guests.

MAY HOUSE

Underscoring his idea that the dinner table should be its
own room—a chapel for reverent family gatherings—Wright
began to embellish his tables to increase their self-sufficiency.
In the Martin, Robie, Boynton, and other important Prairie
houses, lamps and planters appeared at the corners to further
define table edges and avoid messy clutter. For Wright,
elaborate floral arrangements on table tops merely disrupted
the smooth flow of conversation. The relatively modest May
House of 1908 in Grand Rapids, Michigan, was one of the
houses that received a luxurious dining group guarded by
large lamps suspended over plant nests. The whole affair
topped the pillars like classical column capitals. Unlike the
Martin family, which found that its even taller lights interfered
with serving, the Mays kept theirs. Marching down the sides
of the lamps, a simple rectangular motif echoes the art glass
pattern in the dining room windows and throughout the
house. Chevrons in the carpet repeat the cap of the light
shade and reinforce the geometric base of all of Wright's
work, which was executed here by the interior designer
George Niedecken. Even a table runner was part of the
interior package. The chairs, clipped at the top, have solid
backs, not open slats like others of the period. Allowing
no distractions, they help focus diners on the task at hand.

60
.
.
.
.
.
.
.

BOYNTON HOUSE

Wright, the magician, pulled out all of his tricks for the Rochester, New York, dining room of Edward Boynton, a widower who lived with his daughter, Beulah. Susan Lawrence Dana's dining room may have risen to the clouds, but this 1908 Prairie house stretches out as broad and long as one of Wright's dining tables themselves. In this assured room, dinner truly became dining. For two people sharing a house with only a cook and a maid, it was a grand space indeed. To softly brighten the room without glare, "moonlight"—electric light recessed overhead—merges with natural light from wall-to-wall expanses of windows and clerestories. On the major table, light standards stake out the four corners. Lower and quieter than at the May House, their square pattern, like a shoji screen's, mimics the square motifs that energize the glass. Flat backs on the side and arm chairs cant outward ever so slightly, relaxing the required posture for a moment. Nestled in the window-side bower of glass, a smaller table set may have been especially inviting to the two Boyntons when they ate by themselves. Directly across the room is a handsome built-in buffet whose illuminated glass cabinets add the final sleight-of-hand needed to surround the room with magical light.

BOYNTON HOUSE

To serve a spectacular dining environment such as the Boynton
House's required an equally accomplished kitchen. Wright
undoubtedly did not spend much time in kitchens, but
beginning with his own house in Oak Park he devoted due
architectural attention to the "laboratory" in which food was
prepared. His Prairie houses generally had roomy kitchens
near the dining area and sometimes an adjacent pantry. It was
usually a cook—not the lady or gentleman of the house—who
inhabited this backstairs world, as Wright's clients tended to be
successful business and professional people who could afford
hired help. The Boyntons' kitchen is a cozy enclave fairly
typical of the era before kitchens evolved from soothing wood
to high-tech sheen. Pine cabinets line the walls and surround
a practical island occupying the center of the maple floor.
What makes the room only Wright's are the generous windows
outlined by wood bands, displaying the same square motif
found in the elegant dining room beyond. The window
reappears in the pantry next door, where more built-in cabinets
and countertops ease the burdens of entertaining. Because
so many Wright kitchens have been changed for modern
living, the fact that this gem survives in good condition is no
little tribute to preservation-minded owners over the years.

HOLLYHOCK HOUSE

A decade after designing his Prairie-style dining rooms, Wright's architecture was moving forward along with the times. Lifestyles, including meal times, were becoming more informal. At Taliesin, his Wisconsin home begun in 1911, Wright carved out a dining space not in its own room but in a niche at the end of the living room. There it was part of the larger ensemble but separate, without the need for walls. Wright found it easier to shape his own rooms than those of his clients, many of whom were reluctant to give up the formality of dining. For Aline Barnsdall's house atop Olive Hill in Hollywood, designed in 1917 but not begun until 1920, Wright maintained the division. The room, however, opens off the entrance hall, up several steps, and thus gains some of its space from both the entry and the kitchen at the opposite end. Continuing the hollyhock motif that is pervasive throughout the house, the chairs are among Wright's most delightful. Although these seats are straight-backed like his earlier Prairie designs, slats have been forsaken for squares piled upon squares to simulate hollyhocks budding on a stem. At the heart of this floral display is a triangular-based table with a hexagonal top— a shape that can be found in the windows on one side and the doors on the other. They lead out to the garden court, where more hollyhocks, turned to stone, awaited after-dinner strollers.

FALLINGWATER

Both the dining area and the kitchen at Fallingwater are modest in size but not in perspective. They suited the informal weekends the Kaufmann family spent at its wooded retreat in Mill Run, Pennsylvania, and reflected Wright's new way of economizing space beginning in the mid-1930s, when the internationally renowned house first took form. He began calling kitchens "workspaces" and focused them more on no-nonsense labor, just as their new name implied. Fallingwater's kitchen of course was blessed with an incomparable setting, in a valley over a waterfall. Wright used it to full advantage by installing floor-to-ceiling windows even here, edged in red to call attention to the view. Rough sandstone walls inside turn the corner and blend without a trace into the walls outside. Only glass, butted right into the stone, etches a demarcation line. A reminder of the living room hearth, a massive boulder comes indoors here to serve as a ledge for kitchen accouterments. Buff-colored cabinets paint a bright counterpoint to the natural masonry, just as the floating terraces beyond the window enliven the whole of this house cantilevered over falling waters.

SMITH HOUSE

As early as 1896, Wright had defied tradition to suggest that
a dining room might be little more than "a sunny alcove of the
living room." But it took him another four decades to persuade
homeowners that they could live without a separate, formal
room in which to dine. The change flowered with his Usonian
houses, the more economical residences he launched with
the first Jacobs House of 1936 in Madison, Wisconsin. In these
streamlined one-story homes, a dining space was usually tucked
into the niche where the two legs of the L-shaped plan came
together. Without walls, open space flowed freely from one
area to another. In 1950 Sara and Melvyn Maxwell Smith of
Bloomfield Hills, Michigan, were among the fortunate few
who could move into one of these progressive Usonians. Their
snug dining alcove would meld into the living area except
for a half wall that doubles as storage and display. Overhead,
soft light filters down through geometric cutouts typical of
Wright's Usonians, a solution he first devised in his own Oak
Park dining room in 1895. Behind the chairs at left the cutouts
expand to cover an entire wall of screened glass leading to the
terrace. On the other side, the kitchen has become a compact
"workspace"—almost an afterthought as far as homemakers
in many Usonians were concerned. But Wright had made
every foot count and brought his concepts within reach not
only of prosperous business people but also of teachers, as the
Smiths were, and others who shared his adventurous spirit.

USONIAN PAVILION

In 1953 Wright took his vision of Usonia to an unlikely place: New York City. On the site where his Guggenheim Museum now stands, the architect shared his model for modern living with a public vastly greater than the select number of clients he had already won over. In conjunction with an international traveling exhibition of his work entitled *Sixty Years of Living Architecture,* he and his apprentices built the New York Exhibition House, a brick-and-plywood Usonian shell. In its airy, light-filled living area, the business of dining was to take place right in full view, without benefit of walls, screens, or separate nooks. The only buffer was a set of oak plywood chairs whose high backs recalled Wright's preferred seating since the 1895 remodeling of his Oak Park dining room. Their striking geometric cutouts may be read as a kind of Usonian shorthand: a square module, on which this house was designed, nestled in the L shape typical of Usonians, all of it streaking down into a triangular alternative like a bolt of lightning. Clerestory cutouts for the house displayed a similar pattern. Even though this model house has given way to Wright's famous museum, both it and the furniture lived on in Ohio and Iowa, in clones inspired by ideas too good to be temporary.

73

USONIAN PAVILION

Secluded behind a brick wall rising from the dining table in the New York Exhibition House was the "workspace." Unlike many of Wright's Usonian kitchens, this one was more than just a narrow galley hidden away from the life of the house. The natural materials that made the other rooms seem richer than the budget reappeared here to create a sense of seamless unity. No glaring white paint or shiny metal surfaces destroyed the symmetry. Instead, wood-veneered cabinets and shelves rested against brick walls just as in the main room. A circular work island in the center added a playful note while it repeated the lines of the house's furniture. The small but elegant art glass windows of the Boynton House kitchen gave way here to a startling stretch of plate glass reaching from the sinks to the ceiling. The cook would have a fine view. At the age of eighty-six years, Wright had taken the pulse of the American people and prescribed for them a type of house totally fit for life in the modern age.

NOOKS &

Every inglenook and every corner of a home was vital to Wright's overall scheme. Although living and dining rooms received the preponderance of his attention, other spaces shared the "one basic idea" at the heart of each work. The architect's own studios and offices at home, from his first in Oak Park to the last at Taliesin West in Arizona, document his continuous quest

CRANNIES

for new solutions to age-old problems. He tinkered with them so much

that they became architectural laboratories whose discoveries enriched later

clients. Wright's ingenuity was tested as well in designing a hallway, which

in his hands became a mystical loggia, or a terrace bridging the worlds of

indoors and outdoors. For each, the answer lay in simplicity, unity, and nature.

FRANK LLOYD WRIGHT HOME AND STUDIO

By 1895 Frank and Catherine Wright had four children in their growing family. When he remodeled their Oak Park home that year he gave them a gift beyond the means of most fathers: a wonderland of a playroom. The sheer bravado of this upstairs space, entered down a low, compressed hallway, showed that the young architect was heading into uncharted waters. From the entrance a small arch expands exponentially into a rotund barrel vault of a ceiling. Ribs draw concentric rings, interrupted only by recessed center lights laced with a fret-sawn pattern much like the one in the new dining room below. This was a room for serious play—music, drama, books, and Catherine's kindergarten for local children. Audience or actors would climb up to the balcony to see or be seen. Books could be stored in bookcases, toys in built-in storage cabinets under the windows, and art along elevated wood decks that Wright called "eye music." Light enters from bands of bay windows whose simple geometric pattern resembles a tulip. Illuminated squares of light, added after Wright traveled to Japan in 1905, carry the motif right into the room. Over the fireplace rises a mural painted by Orlando Giannini that brings to life the tale "The Fisherman and the Genie" from the *Arabian Nights*. The fisherman is depicted realistically, but the genie, distilled to its geometric essence, is a portent of things to come from Wright's hand. In photographs, this tour de force of a room looms larger than life, probably a trick Wright intended. But the windows sit low on short cabinets; the fireplace is tall; and the ceiling drops down to fool adults. In reality, it is meant to be seen through children's eyes.

YE'VE LEFT A GLIMMER STILL TO CHEER
THE MAN ~ THE ARTIFEX
THAT HOLDS IN SPITE O' KNOCKS AND SCALE
O' FRICTION WASTE AN' SLIP,
AN' BY THAT LIGHT ~ NOW MARK MY WORD ~
WE'LL BUILD THE PERFECT SHIP.

FRANK LLOYD WRIGHT HOME AND STUDIO

In 1898 Wright decided to put his work and his home under one roof in Oak Park. Attached by a narrow passageway near the study of the expanded house, a new studio complex—drafting room, library, office, and reception hall—was just what an up-and-coming architect needed to announce his calling to the world. As was his practice, Wright experimented with the studio just as he did with the house. A new entry, an ethereal skylight, and other alterations took place over the next decade even as Wright and his associates turned out more than one hundred fifty commissions during his busiest Prairie-style years. The center of all this activity was the two-level drafting room, where lines from Rudyard Kipling encouraged the crew to "build the perfect ship." A nautical-looking balcony above the main workroom carries through the analogy. Suspended from the octagonal roof by iron chains, this octagonal deck floats over the square room in a masterful geometric counterpoint. Decorative arts designers worked up here, the architects below. Between them, sculptures and models would rest on intersecting timbers that served as shelves. Natural light floods the space from mostly clear glass on both levels, aided by balloonlike bulbs and task lighting over the drafting tables. It was a new space for Wright's new age of architecture.

FRANK LLOYD WRIGHT HOME AND STUDIO

When Wright's clients climbed the steps to his Oak Park studio and entered his reception hall after 1898, they knew that they were in the presence of greatness. Past whimsical sculptures of storks, beneath an arbor of green and gold art glass, they were ushered into the architect's inner sanctum. The studio library, where they met, is as octagonal as the drafting room is square—as if the grown-up child had scattered his Froebel blocks until the shapes pleased him. The windows are high, to provide light but prevent distractions from the business of reviewing plans. Artificial light comes from a large skylight of clear glass. More glass appears in a built-in cabinet, which is flanked by cork panels on which drawings could be displayed. Room for art was not forgotten: ledges provide perches for some of Wright's collection of art pottery, Japanese ware, and dried flowers to bring nature indoors. It was a deliberate stage set certain to let prospective clients know that they could have a building as progressive as their architect's.

MARTIN HOUSE

Nature suffused the grand Prairie house Wright designed
in 1904 for Darwin and Isabel Martin of Buffalo, New York,
both nature lovers like Wright. A conservatory reached
via a pergola from the main house brought greenery inside.
Broad planters offered bouquets near the front door.
Feathered friends were even accommodated in innovative
concrete birdhouses. But the most famous of his nature
designs for the house are incised in glass, which Wright saw
as thin sheets of air—almost crystal. Windows in a stylized
pattern called the Tree of Life greet visitors in the reception
hall and ring the upper stories like a forest. In the atrium here
one set peeks out over an oak-screened balcony. From a square
base, its stalks rise to hold chevrons of leaves or branches, all
rendered in Wright's finest geometry with iridescent glass
chosen to change colors as day changes to night. For modern
buildings, he disliked pictorial stories in glass that interfered
with the view; instead, suggested Wright, designs should
acknowledge the flatness of glass and stay "severely 'put'."

MAY HOUSE

As early as 1894, Wright was asking why the second floor of
a house should be less carefully planned than the first. Pay
attention to yourself and not just to the neighbors, he told
homeowners, and make the "sleeping rooms" as pleasant as
the living room and a natural outgrowth of it. In the 1908 May
House in Grand Rapids, Michigan, the masterful downstairs
themes make the climb upstairs. The color scheme and several
key features closely link the master bedroom to the public
areas of the house. Art glass windows wrap around a corner
to replace a wall, inviting light and nature inside. Through the
geometry of cubes and chevrons, they portray wheat growing
in a field. A fireplace, flecked with gilded mortar, is clearly
a pair to the one in the living room, only a little less imposing.
Wood bands snake around the room at ceiling level to tie it
all together. Simple bedsteads, one an original designed by
Wright, the other a copy, carry though the rectilinear motif.
Overhead, the ceiling has become a peaked canopy to suggest
a decided sense of shelter. In this house at least, the underwear
(to use the architect's analogy) was as handsome as the outer-
wear, and both the owners and the neighbors could be pleased.

STORER HOUSE

California offered a far more hospitable climate for building with nature than the Midwest. Beginning with his early houses, however, Wright had invited the outside in through terraces and banks of windows—with warm weather in shorter supply on the prairie, the need was even greater. The Golden State, where Wright built five houses in the 1920s, begged for outdoor living nearly year-round. In the Hollywood home designed for John Storer in 1923, the architect was quick to oblige. Terraces with shrubbery designed by his son Lloyd Wright greet visitors at the ground level. More garden terraces open up the main floor, while the living room on the treetop level sits snugly between two terraces that cross it like a T. Square-patterned textile-block walls provide a backdrop in these transition spaces just as they do inside. Textured like foliage and layered one block atop another, the concrete houses were meant to stand like trees amid nature's real forests, and they do. Shade comes from a colorful canopy of geometric awnings raised on redwood posts and spiked with copper finials. When drawings for these whimsical terrace parasols were recently discovered by the current owner, they were installed with the assistance of Eric Lloyd Wright. His father, Lloyd, had been left to contend with the problems of building these innovative houses while his own father worked in Japan. Now the third generation of architects in the Wright family is restoring the work of both the father and the grandfather.

ENNIS HOUSE

How one got from one place to another was important to
the theatrical bent in Wright's personality. Drama flourished
in many of his entries—a purposely low ceiling could explode
into a soaring room just a few steps beyond. He liked to
compress, then release space to keep things lively, adding
surprises along with complexity. A seemingly endless loggia,
or hallway, offers the same dramatic touch in Mabel and
Charles Ennis's 1923 house in Los Angeles. A latter-day Mayan
temple, it was the grandest of Wright's textile-block designs.
Square-within-a-square motifs inscribe what could be
prehistoric pictographs from wall to wall and column to
column. The loggia runs nearly the length of the interior, past
dining room, living room, and bedroom, and leads to terraces
on either side. It is solemn but serene, inviting the same
reverence as a monastic courtyard. Release comes in the form
of a window above, dressed in the details of Wright's old
Prairie-style patterns—one of a number of alterations made to
the house over his objections. The concrete houses were meant
to be a new way of building, and he had moved beyond his
old standbys. The shiny marble floor, lacking the artlessness of
natural materials, never would have been a Wright choice.

TALIESIN WEST

One of the first permanent buildings constructed to launch Taliesin West beginning in 1937 was the drafting studio. Even though they had come to the Arizona desert to escape the harsh Wisconsin winters, Wright and his Taliesin Fellowship had work to do. First he assigned his apprentices the task of building the studio, a long, narrow space roomy enough for his thirty students. Back in Wisconsin the apprentices worked in "an abstract forest" of triangle posts brought down to table height, but in the sunny West the triangle was inverted. Ribbed in redwood, it soars in the studio from low windows to high clerestories—a mountain of a space as inspiring as the McDowell peaks forming Taliesin West's back yard. The apprentices set local boulders into forms with sandy cement to recycle the desert into novel stone walls. What they built has been described as a glorified tent, one made of canvas panels on hinged frames. In rain or shine, these could be closed for protection or opened to invite the desert breezes inside. Natural canvas provided just the soft, nonglaring light from above that Wright liked. But canvas leaked and became discolored. When it proved too ephemeral, the original covering was replaced by plastic panels that offer much the same delicate translucence. Never far away in his office, Wright would come to the studio up to 1959, in his ninety-second year. His hat parked on a ledge, he was always ready to work.

PUBLIC

Wright liked to say that his interest in architecture stretched from the

chicken coop to the cathedral. Just as he gave new form to houses, he called

for new ways of seeing the public spaces in which people work, worship, and

entertain themselves. No more churches in Gothic garb, no banks as Greek

temples, no French châteaux for anything. Few public buildings gave him

SPACES

as much pleasure as theaters—he could put his own dramatic personality on

stage—although he addressed every commission with the zeal of an innovator.

Offices allowed him to design for a larger family of workers, religious build-

ings to express his innate reverence for nature. Public clients were not as

numerous or adventurous as homeowners, but each received a masterwork.

LARKIN BUILDING

Wright called this office building in Buffalo, New York, "the first emphatic protest in architecture"—but today we have little more than photographs with which to judge. Completed in 1906, it did not last half a century and was gone by 1950. But even in two dimensions, the interior of this "simple cliff of brick" stands as one of Wright's most awe-inspiring spaces, especially considering how early in his career it came. The entire building looked inward, turning its back on an ugly urban site. Workers in the mail-order company—its "great official family"—were pampered with a central court that dispensed sunshine from a skylighted rooftop five stories above. Wright was able to free up this unobstructed space—he saw it as a single large room—by removing the stairs and mechanical systems to the corners of the massive square building. Office "galleries" surrounded the atrium, in which some people also worked. On the fifth-floor level, Wright inscribed homilies around the cream-colored court to urge the employees to excel. In lieu of classical acanthus leaves, mammoth capitals sported geometric blocks that flowered into globes of light. For a company whose main product was soap, Wright dedicated himself to wholesomeness and the welfare of the Larkin workers who used the building daily. Metal chairs were designed to ease both the sitters' posture and the evening cleanup. Toilets were cantilevered from walls so that mops could easily scrub underneath. A conservatory and flower boxes added nature to compensate for the lack of nurturing scenery outside. Watched over by Wright's *Winged Victory*, the Larkin Building was an astounding achievement clearly marked by Intelligence, Enthusiasm, and Control.

UNITY TEMPLE

What Wright was striving for in the Larkin Building he fully
accomplished at Unity Temple. For this Unitarian church in
Oak Park, Illinois, completed the same year, the hometown
architect allowed the congregation's needs to shape the
whole, letting "the room inside be the architecture outside."
Here the reality of the building became its space within.
Wright moved structural supports in from the corners and
cantilevered the roof, freeing up non-load-bearing walls for
windows and thereby destroying the box. He was helped by a
pliable new material—reinforced concrete—which he poured
and left unadorned like flesh on bones to form two cubical
structures, a large one for worship and a smaller one for
communal activities. Wright later prophesied that his exteriors
would shock the public more than his interiors because
they stemmed from such a radically different idea of what
a building should be. Outside and inside, Unity Temple
continues to startle nearly a century after it opened in 1906.
In this wholly modern meeting house, members enter the
auditorium to find an unencumbered space flooded with light
from skylights overhead; high art glass windows behind the
pulpit and above balconies on both sides echo the ceiling
coffers and the square plan of the structure itself. In low-
hanging lamps, spheres vary the rectilinear motifs that extend
to the organ screen and wood bands edging most surfaces.
Growing from the needs of the building, the ornament is
completely integrated and organic. Simplicity became the
means to the end. Wright had finally set architecture free.

COONLEY PLAYHOUSE

Wright joked that he was always proud to have a client survive his first building and return for another, and it happened only a handful of times. Among his happy repeat clients were Queene and Avery Coonley, for whom Wright had designed an expansive Prairie house in Riverside, Illinois, in 1907. A proponent of kindergartens and other means of progressive education, Queenie Coonley sponsored a number of schools and decided to build one on their property. In 1912 Wright produced an assured concrete cube of a building that became known as the Coonley Playhouse because children were encouraged to give dramatic performances on its stage. As they did so, they were surrounded by some of the most joyous art glass of Wright's career—perhaps because it is, appropriately, so childlike. The inspiration, he admitted, came from the balloons and confetti of small-town parades. Circles, semicircles, squares, rectangles, and even a few American flags shower the room with playfulness from clerestories overhead and a triptych framed by sidelights. Forecasting Mondrian, the motifs are abstract, like the new art Wright may have seen during his stay in Europe in 1909–10. The patterns are scattered asymmetrically, and the colors are surprisingly primary—both departures from Wright's usual nature-based symmetry and palette. This experiment motivated Wright a few years later to pull out more balloon shapes for a mural at Midway Gardens in Chicago and tableware for the Imperial Hotel in Tokyo. Although the original Coonley Playhouse windows were removed many years ago, new owners have authentically reproduced them as part of their restoration of the building. They have even furnished their new living area with tables and chairs that poignantly recall its educational legacy.

MIDWAY GARDENS

Wright designed many outdoor rooms in his long career—
terraces, pergolas, even a birdwalk—but his grandest enclo-
sure of nature took place in downtown Chicago at Midway
Gardens. Some thought it was only a beer hall, but using
concrete and brick and geometric shapes remembered from
childhood Froebel blocks, he composed a symphony melding
architecture, art, sculpture, furnishings, landscape design, music,
and dance—"a festival for the eyes" just as music was for the
ears. It was designed in 1913 to emulate outdoor restaurants
popular in Europe. A Winter Garden with a balconied dining
room and a bar inside made allowances for bad weather,
but when Midway opened in the summer of 1914 most of the
excitement was outdoors, in the Summer Garden. Cubistic
sprites by Alfonso Iannelli hovered over stepped terraces filled
with tables and chairs for seven hundred plus room for dancing.
A band shell stood opposite the Winter Garden, while wings
spread out at the ends with more balconies from which to join
the open-air fun. Countering the great horizontality, towers
and light fixtures reached for the sky. Everywhere, Wright's
trusty T-square, triangle, and compass drew magic with squares,
triangles, and circles. In *City by the Sea*, a pair of murals, he
brought the parade indoors with a battalion of balloons
reminiscent of the Coonley Playhouse windows. Some of his
decorative designs were never executed, as the show lasted
only two years. Bankrupt, Midway became a real beer garden
until Prohibition and then changed so much that Wright
himself wished for its demise. In 1929 his wish was granted.

JOHNSON WAX
BUILDING

At first the state building code staff did not believe that
the columns—tapering down to near pinpoints—could
withstand the designated loads. So Wright called their bluff.
After his hollow columns, made of poured concrete over
wire mesh, withstood sixty tons, or five times the required
weight, he got his building permit and work began on the
Johnson Wax Administration Building in Racine, Wisconsin.
When the three-story headquarters finally opened in 1939,
"We became a different company," proclaimed its chairman.
This was certainly true of the employees, for whom Wright
designed a cathedral meant to be as inspiring as any house
of worship. In the main workroom, the Johnson Wax staff
still toils in an indoor garden filled with those sturdy columns,
whose lily-pad tops stretch eighteen feet across. At the third
level, the lilies rise to skylights and support the roof, thus
freeing the perimeter of the rectangular structure for another
gift of light. At the cornice line Wright wrapped coils of
Pyrex tubing to bring the outside in. These rivers of glass hide
distractions of the site, helping the building turn inward just
as the Larkin Building did before it. Colors and shapes are
seamlessly integrated throughout: The circular motif of the
column tops reappears in round backs and seats on the chairs,
which are the same red as the bricks of this building and a
companion tower added in 1944. Desks also gently round at
the edges as they cantilever outward. Aluminum piping on
chairs and desks resembles the glass tubing. Now that Wright's
tottering three-legged chairs have been converted to four
legs, this forest of industry seems destined to survive and thrive.

PFEIFFER CHAPEL

Because Wright designed few schools, the opportunity
in 1938 to design an entire campus was one he could not
pass up. At Florida Southern College in Lakeland, his task
was to transform a lakeside orange grove into an academic
community of about sixteen structures. Building here without
much help from nature, Wright devised a series of structures
linked by esplanades poised on triangular points. For his
material he chose concrete blocks, as he had in California in
the 1920s, but formed them of sand and coquina shells to give
the campus a luster finished by the Florida sunshine. The first
order of business for the Methodist institution was a student
chapel. Built in 1940 and named for Annie Merner Pfeiffer,
this pioneer structure is an elongated hexagon on a rectangle.
As its signature feature, Wright turned a conventional steeple
into a bell tower of masonry and glass, glimpses of which—
snaking its way skyward in triangles—can be caught from
inside the sanctuary. Light envelops this space above from
windows and skylights and below from a mosaic of colored
glass cut into the blocks. For the choir loft Wright wove
a lacy filigree of concrete and pierced it as a reminder of the
chapel's hexagonal plan. Unlike most Wright buildings, the
exterior does not fully foretell the majesty of the space inside.

UNITARIAN
MEETING HOUSE

By 1947 Wright had found a way to express reverence
without using a clichéd steeple or a tower as he had at Florida
Southern. For this church in a suburb of Madison, Wisconsin,
he simply turned the building into a steeple—a triangle
of aspiration that rises from the ground like two hands raised
in prayer. Deep under the overhang of the copper roof,
a window wall thrusts out to touch nature and make it part
of the congregation. In front of it rises the pulpit, stacked with
the same limestone that clads the exterior as well as the walls
of Wright's Taliesin not far away. A balcony accommodates
the choir, sheltered by a baffle to direct their voices out into
the auditorium along with the notes of the organ behind
them. The deeply sloped plaster ceiling also recalls Taliesin's,
smooth against rough stone, but here it sparkles with
starry inset lights. Opposite the soaring pulpit is an equally
impressive fireplace, the centerpiece of a space that can
be partitioned off as needed. Low wings on either side of
the pentagonal auditorium hold offices and rooms for Sunday
school and meetings. Wright, who was raised a Unitarian,
proclaimed that the meeting house expressed the unity at
the heart of the members' beliefs—not to mention his own.

MORRIS GIFT SHOP

Late in Wright's career circles occupied his mind far beyond the two-dimensional art glass patterns and murals he had played with earlier on. More and more he brought them to life in three dimensions. His first design for the Guggenheim Museum in New York City, prepared in 1943, presented a novel ziggurat whose interior ramp spiraled downward in the cause of art. Although Fifth Avenue did not finally get its museum until 1959, the spiral remained alive in Wright's imagination. It popped back into consciousness when he was asked in 1948 to remodel a store off Union Square in San Francisco for the V. C. Morris family. The exterior gives few clues as to what awaits inside. No walls of commercial plate glass for Wright—he clad the facade in austere Roman brick. All that marks the entrance is a run of inset square lights pointing to a deeply recessed archway. Once through the door, one could have stumbled into a West Coast Guggenheim, albeit squatter. A ramp gently moves browsers to the second level, past portholes, semicircles, and dangling spherical cutouts in the wall that offer light and spots for display. Where the sky might be, clouds of fluffy spheres reinforce the building's circular scheme. Sets of four semicircles each mark the edges of larger, flatter circles of glass as delicate as the glassware and china originally shown here. The artwork that has replaced them only increases the store's resemblance to the Guggenheim. In both spaces, Wright used a circle to eliminate the square and thereby destroyed the box.

HILLSIDE THEATRE

Theaters presented Wright with a natural stage for his dramatic inclinations. From the Coonley Playhouse for children of 1912, he moved on to create one for his own students after he and his new wife, Olgivanna, established the Taliesin Fellowship in 1932. For this he chose to convert the gymnasium of the second Hillside Home School, which he had designed for his aunts in 1902 on the Taliesin property. Once the Hillside Playhouse was completed in 1933, the Wrights and the apprentices enjoyed two decades of concerts, movies, and some performances to which the public was invited. But in 1952 Taliesin's third fire destroyed this wing of the Fellowship complex. By the next year it was back, in altered but improved form. On the wall, Walt Whitman's advice on wisdom was relettered, but Wright reworked the seating into a cozy L formation that embraces the stage. Rectilinear wooden seats gave way to playful disks of red metal recalling the Johnson Wax Building chairs. On stage, at the third leg of the triangle, the striking theater curtain was reborn—a work of both art and craft. Like Wright's art glass of old, it tells a story of nature in his own geometric language. The tale describes the land around Taliesin:its brown fields, its red barns, its green hills, over all of which blackbirds fly. Hand appliquéd of felt on linen, the curtain pulled together the room as well as the life of the eighty-five-year-old architect.

BETH SHOLOM SYNAGOGUE

Wright announced in the 1950s that the church he attended was Nature with a capital *N*. Not belonging to any one church, he felt free to design all manner of religious buildings. For the Beth Sholom congregation just outside Philadelphia in Elkins Park, Pennsylvania, the nature worshiper conjured up a mountain of glass in 1954. The building, responded its rabbi, was Mount Sinai itself. Roughly hexagonal in plan, almost a triangle, it rises like a pyramid dressed in glass outside and neutral fiberglass inside. The main sanctuary is thus sheltered all around by light, as if, said Wright, it were tucked into the hands of God. He achieved this incomparable sense of space by suspending a steel tripod frame from the topmost point a hundred feet up and anchoring it in concrete at ground level. One thousand seats slope toward the dais and, behind it, the Ark holding the Torah. Emphatically restating the synagogue's geometric motif, a triangular chandelier of glass explodes color over the congregants. Smaller triangles zigzag through concrete like the bands of wood in Wright's Prairie houses a half century earlier. Outside, seven triangular vessels climb each of the building's three ridges—abstract menorahs that further light the way.

ANNUNCIATION GREEK ORTHODOX CHURCH

Wright burrowed partly underground for his next great
church, for the Greek Orthodox community of Wauwatosa,
Wisconsin, a Milwaukee suburb. In this 1956 design he
returned to the circle but flattened it outside into a low blue
dome redolent of the Middle East. Under the roof lies the
main sanctuary, a circular, two-level room that rests on four
curved concrete piers forming a Greek cross within the
circular plan. This sanctuary stands alone, a perfect disk for
the world to see, because other church activities are placed
out of sight below ground. Eyebrow windows filled with
stained glass bring in light over the balcony, from which
it filters down to the main level and mixes with globes of
artificial light. Around the altar, a screen of gold-anodized
aluminum bears more encircled crosses and puts the final golden
touch on the space. Circles scribe their magic at every turn.
The three sets of stairs even spiral from one level to the other,
giving churchgoers the choice of resting in the security of the
lower space or rising to the celestial pleasures of the dome.

GUGGENHEIM MUSEUM

Wright never thought much of pictures in the home—he said that they defaced the walls—but he did favor sculpture in three dimensions, much as his own work was. In conceiving the plan for a museum of modern art in Manhattan, his thoughts turned to urban sculpture. He would give Solomon R. Guggenheim a masterpiece both simple—like an egg shell—and radical—one continuous spiral of space from top to bottom. The Guggenheim has never been without controversy. In his own day, sixteen years elapsed before it was actually opened in 1959, and by then Wright had died. Today many critics still complain that the architecture interferes with the art, whereas Wright thought that most art was superfluous in his architecture. What is undeniable is that he took lowly concrete, the "gutter-rat" that had challenged him for fifty years, and shaped it into a temple. In his hands, it was plastic. It flowed into a ziggurat of concentric circles that stream upward until stopped by a dodecagonal dome of glass. At this pinnacle museum visitors are expected to begin their promenade, strolling down the gentle ramp to exit where they entered. The viewers always know their place within the central rotunda, and they know where the art is—not secreted in far-off corners of the building, enclosed within four walls. Wright revived the idea of the spiral a number of times over his career but never with such daring as he persevered in achieving in the heart of New York City.

MARIN COUNTY CIVIC CENTER

Public officials tended to shy away from the outspoken Wright, so it was a rarity when he won the commission in 1957 to design a county government center outside San Francisco. He was then in his ninetieth year and did not live to see its Administration Building opened in 1962 or the complex completed with the Hall of Justice in 1969. The center's two arms, 584 and 880 feet long respectively, stretch over its hilly site like an arcaded aqueduct erected by ancient Rome. They join in the middle at a low-domed library, its blue roof not unlike Wright's Greek Orthodox Church in Wisconsin. This sprawling horizontality is punctuated only by a tall antenna tower decked out in Wrightian geometry. Befitting the California location, an outdoor room seemed called for. But this being northern California, a roof—however transparent— was needed. Wright reached back into his past and pulled out a great barrel vault, this time clad in a mere sheet of crystal to coax light into all corners. Encouraging views to reach to the clouds, the skylighted atrium, called the mall, travels the full length of each building, ending just outside the county jail. Planted with greenery, the space brings the garden indoors. Wright ended as he began: building with nature.

SELECTED BIBLIOGRAPHY

Guerrero, Pedro E. *Picturing Wright: An Album from Frank Lloyd Wright's Photographer.* San Francisco: Pomegranate, 1994.

Hanks, David A. *The Decorative Designs of Frank Lloyd Wright.* New York: Dutton, 1979.

——. *Frank Lloyd Wright: Preserving an Architectural Heritage. Decorative Designs from The Domino's Pizza Collection.* New York: Dutton, 1989.

Harrington, Elaine. *Frank Lloyd Wright Home and Studio, Oak Park.* Stuttgart: Edition Axel Menges, 1996.

Hitchcock, Henry-Russell. *In the Nature of Materials: The Buildings of Frank Lloyd Wright, 1887–1941.* 1942. Reprint, New York: Da Capo, 1969.

Kaufmann, Edgar, Jr. *Fallingwater: A Frank Lloyd Wright Country House.* New York: Abbeville, 1986.

Lind, Carla. *Lost Wright: Frank Lloyd Wright's Vanished Masterpieces.* New York: Simon and Schuster, 1996.

——. *Wright at a Glance Series.* 12 vols. San Francisco: Pomegranate: 1994–96.

——. *The Wright Style.* New York: Simon and Schuster, 1992.

Pfeiffer, Bruce Brooks. *Frank Lloyd Wright.* 1991. Reprint, New York: Barnes and Noble Books, 1994

——. *Frank Lloyd Wright: The Masterworks.* New York: Rizzoli, 1993.

Secrest, Meryle. *Frank Lloyd Wright.* New York: Knopf, 1992.

Storrer, William Allin. *The Frank Lloyd Wright Companion.* Chicago: University of Chicago Press, 1993.

Waggoner, Lynda S. *Fallingwater: Frank Lloyd Wright's Romance with Nature.* New York: Universe, 1996.

Wright, Frank Lloyd. *Frank Lloyd Wright: Collected Writings.* 5 vols. Edited by Bruce Brooks Pfeiffer. New York: Rizzoli, 1992–95.

PHOTOGRAPHERS

This book is dedicated to my dear colleagues Pedro E. Guerrero and Balthazar Korab and the other photographers below who are able to interpret the work of Frank Lloyd Wright beyond the power of words:

Art Institute of Chicago, Ryerson and Burnham Libraries: 105, 106–7

Judith Bromley: 16–17, 52, 102–3

Buffalo and Erie County Historical Society, Larkin Collection: 98

Doug Carr, courtesy Dana-Thomas House: 56–57

Richard Cheek: 39

Frank Lloyd Wright Home and Studio Foundation: Endpapers, 10–11, 48–49, 76–77, 96–97

Jeff Goldberg/Esto: 123

Farrell Grehan: 109, 110–11

Pedro E. Guerrero: 9, 22, 46–47, 72–73, 75, 94–95, 116–17, 120–21

Biff Henrich/Keystone Film Productions: 86

Balthazar Korab: 6, 18–19, 42–43, 55, 58–59, 70, 101, 113, 118

Andrew D. Lautman: 44–45

Christopher Little: 32–33, 68–69

Paul E. Loven: 36–37

Jon Miller/Hedrich Blessing: 2, 12, 14–15, 51, 79, 80–81, 82

Andrew Olenick/Fotowerks: 62–63, 65

Cervin Robinson: 24–25

Steelcase Inc.: 20–21, 60–61, 88–89

Ezra Stoller/Esto: 35, 40–41

Tim Street-Porter: 28–29, 30–31, 66–67, 91, 92

Alexander Vertikoff: 26–27

Scot Zimmerman: 114–15, 124

INDEX

127